BENARES ILLUSTRATED

IN

A SERIES OF DRAWINGS

JAMES PRINSEP

ESQ. F.R.S.

GYAN

Published by

GYAN

Gyan Publishing House
5, Ansari Road
Daryaganj, New Delhi-110002
Phone: 011-47034999, 9811692060
E-mail: books@gyanbooks.com

Distribution Network
gyanbooks.com
India, USA, Canada, UK, Australia, France

ISBN: 978-81-212-8302-1 (PB)

First Published, 1831

2nd Impression 2023

Printed at: Gyan Press, Delhi.

BENARES ILLUSTRATED
Author: JAMES PRINSEP

CONTENTS

BENARES ILLUSTRATED

JAMES PRINSEP

LIST OF ILLUSTRATORS

PREFACE

THE City of BENARES has long been known to Europe as the principal seat of Hindoo learning and superstition, and as the stronghold of the Brahminical faith in modern times. Its extent and importance have been magnified in all ages, and its wonders depicted in colors far too vivid to be correct. But it has always possessed enough of real attraction to the curious in Indian manners and literature, and deservedly, therefore, occupies a prominent place in the relations of Indian travellers. Amongst others of less note, the descriptions of TAVERNIER and HEBER will long continue to be read with interest:— the former, as a lively picture of Benares in 1608, before the prostration of its temples by AURUNGZEBE, and while there yet remained some vestiges of the splendor of its idolatries; the latter, as introducing the reader, in the amiable prelate's agreeable and instructive manner, to Benares, as it appeared to him on his visit in 1625.

The pencil, though not entirely idle, has hitherto done little to bring the Holy City to the notice of Europe. Sketches of the place, as viewed from the river, are indeed to be found in the volumes *both* of HEBER and LORD VALENTIA; but they are executed with little either of minuteness or of fidelity. A fine drawing of *Dusaswumedh Ghât* is also to be *met* with in the magnificent Oriental Portfolio of DANIELL : but these detached views convey to the European reader a very faint idea of the town and its population,—certainly not enough to satisfy curiosity regarding a place which exhibits a larger remnant of the external characteristics of Hindoo taste and habits, than is to be met with in any other Eastern city within the pale of British dominion.

The specimens here presented to the public have no pretension to vie with the works of professional art, by which the cities of Europe have been illustrated. The collection of them amused a portion of the leisure of a ten years' official residence upon the spot; and they were intended, with several others, and a Map of the city, to illustrate the labors of a literary friend, whom other important duties have diverted from the present execution of his design. The only merit aimed at, has been that of faithful delineation. The Map was published in 1824: the views were produced in three series at considerable intervals, owing to the necessity of sending the original drawings to England to be executed in lithography under the charge of a relation, to whose interested exertions, the author is mainly indebted for their appearance before the world. The absence of a correcting hand, acquainted with the peculiarities of Indian costume and scenery, will account for some small errors which a critical eye may detect in several of the representations.

Some of the Plates have been engraved in Calcutta, and although very inferior to the advanced productions of the art at home, still it is hoped they will give a favorable idea of the capabilities of native artists.

A brief explanation accompanies each Plate; but for the benefit of those not conversant with the subject, it has been deemed convenient to preface the whole with a few general observations on the antiquity, history, and population of the town.

INTRODUCTION

VARANASI, or BENARES, (or to be orthoepically correct, according to the system of Dr. Gilchrist, Bunarus,) derives its name from two streams, the *Burna* and *Ussee,* which bound it on the north-east and south-west. Its ancient denomination was KASHEE, "the Splendid," whereof the fabulous wonders are fully detailed in the *Kashee-Khund,* one of the chapters of the *Skundu-Poorana.*

According to this mythological history, *Kashee* is a place of the most profound antiquity, sanctity and splendor: it has survived in age a hundred lives of BRUHMA, each of whose days is equal to 4320 millions of years; it stands apart from the earth, supported upon the *trisool* or trident of MAHADEO, never shaken by earthquakes; and the whole city was once of pure gold, but has since degenerated into stone and brick, along with the rapid deterioration of human virtue. At the period of universal dissolution, *Benares* is unharmed, never being abandoned by SHIVA, from which it derives another of its appellations, of frequent occurrence in the *Pooranas,* or *Avimukta.*

Seeing how little this description is reconcileable with the actual state of things, some learned Natives hold that the *Kashee,* spoken of in the *Pooránas,* never had a physical existence, or local habitation on earth, but that a resemblance only has been attempted by the Brahmuns, in order to incorporate, before the eyes of the pious, the chief of the million epithets or attributes of MAHADEO for their adoration. According to some of the *Pooránas* even, the genuine Benares is invisible in every *Kali* age.

The following succinct notice of the legendary history of the city, is the contribution of a friend, to whose research and accurate knowledge of Sanskrit lore the literary world is already much indebted :—

"The historical traditions concur in assigning a remote date to the origin of *Kási.* The actual period of its foundation, or the name of its founder, is not specified,—in deference, perhaps, to the mythological legends of its antiquity; but it is to be inferred from the list of the kings of *Kási,* found in several *Puránas,* that it owed its rise to a branch of the lunar line of kings, whose dominions extended to the *Doáb* or *Antarvèdi,* and whose capital was *Pratishthána,* at the confluence of the Ganges and Jumna. Of this family, AYUS, the son of PURURAVAS, the grandson of SOMA or the moon, had several sons: the elder continued to reign at *Pratishthána,* but the second, KSHETRAVRIDDHI, was the first of the *Kási* branch. It seems probable, however, that the city was founded not by him, but by his grandson or great grandson, denominated KÁSA and KÁSIRÁJA.

"From twenty-three to twenty-five princes are enumerated in this line, several of whom hold a conspicuous place in Hindu tradition. The grandson of Kásirája was DHANWANTARI, the physician of the gods, produced originally at the churning of the ocean, but subsequently born us man, sovereign of *Kási,* and father of medical science. Works attributed to him and to his pupil SUSRUTA still exist, and concur with the legends to render it likely that Benares was once a celebrated school of medicine amongst the Hindus.

"The third from DHANWANTARI, DIVODÁSA, is still more celebrated; as in his time *Kási* was the seat of a religious revolution, in which the faith of BUDDHA superceded the worship of SIVA. The legends that are told on this subject vary, but the main purport is the same. SIVA, deprived of his residence in Benares by the immaculate purity of the king, in consequence of which the presence of the gods was no longer needed, had no means of recovering his favourite city but the seduction of DIVODÁSA into heresy: for this purpose, NÁREDA, or according to some accounts, VISHNU, came in the character of a *Saugata* or *Buddha* mendicant to Benares, and converted the king to his doctrines. The virtues of DIVODÁSA being thus tainted with heretical notions, the gods returned to earth, and SIVA resumed his station in *Kasi*. It should seem, therefore, that the doctrines of BUDDHA were not at this time permanently triumphant.

"There is no account of the circumstances under which the dynasty of KSHETRAVRIDDHI ended, nor of the family or individuals that succeeded. The line should terminate long before the days of RÁMA, and the principality may have become part of the kingdom of *Ayodhyá*. It is believed, however, that no mention of *Kási* occurs in the *Rámáyana,* which looks as if it was a place of no note when that poem was written. There is no occasion for its introduction, it is true; and perhaps any allusion to a *Saiva* shrine might have been thought inconsistent with the plan of a poem, the hero of which is VISHNU in the form of RÁMA.

"In the *Mahábhárat* frequent mention of *Kási* occurs. The daughter of one king, not named in the usual lists, SARVASENA, is said to have been married to BHARATA, the son of SACUNTALÁ, and emperor of all India. At a later period the daughters of the king of *Kási,* AMBIKÁ and AMBÁLIKÁ, were carried off by BHISHMA as wives for his half-brother VICHITRAVIRYA, and they gave birth to DHRITARÁSHTRA and PÁNDU, between whose sons the sanguinary conflict, which forms the main subject of the *Mahábhárat,* took place.

"Shortly after this, it appears that Benares was destroyed, apparently in a religious war between the *Vaishnavas* and *Saivas,* According to the legendary accounts, a prince named PAUNDRAKA assumed the name and attributes of the son of VASUDEVA, and denounced KRISHNA as an impostor. He was supported chiefly by the Raja of *Kási,* but he and bis ally were defeated and slain by the prince of *Dwáraká.* The son of Kásirája had recourse to SIVA, by whose favour a magical personage was produced, by which Krishna was immediately assailed. KRISHNA directed his *chakra* or discus to defend him, and this weapon not only repelled the enemy, but whirled into Benares, which it set on fire, and the prince and people perished in the conflagration. This story, not improbably, shadows a real transaction."

From the supposed date of the events recorded in the *Mahábhárat,* a long interval of darkness succeeds. That Benares or rather *Káshi* was a city of note in the commencement of the Christian era, may be inferred from the *Cassida,* or *Cassidia (Kási Devi* or *Kási-divyá, Kási* the divine,) which has a place in PTOLEMY'S tables. In the map it is placed not very much out of its actual position, and in a relation to *Conogyza* or *Kanouj,* which approaches to accuracy. It is situated, however, very erroneously with regard to the Ganges, lying not on that river, but on a communicating branch considerably to the east. There can, nevertheless, be little doubt that *Kási* is intended, and we need not be surprised at any errors or omissions in the geography of this part of India, as the Ganges was the utmost limit of the personal knowledge of the ancients, and, as ARRIAN observes, few of them had penetrated even to that boundary.

Of the political state of *Káshi* nothing further is known until the eleventh century. According to some of the Mohammedan accounts, it was governed by a Raja BUNAR at the time of one of MAHMOOD'S invasions, or in A. D. 1017, when one of his generals penetrated to the province, and defeated the Raja. The Ayeen Akburee asserts, that MAHMOOD himself advanced to Benares and made some converts. On the other hand, no mention of the conquest of Benares by MAHMOOD or his officers occurs in *Ferishta,* nor in the authorities consulted by Colonel STEWART.

From these it appears that MAHMOOD'S victories in this direction were limited to Kanouj, from whence he directed his march to Muttra and the west bank of the Jumna, and that his subsequent progress ever after followed a south-westerly course. It appears also, that in 1027 Benares was part of the kingdom of Gour, then governed by MAHI-PÁLA, descended from BHUPÁLA; and that two princes, the sons or brothers of the former, STHIRAPÁLA and VASANTAPÁLA, presided over the city, and impaired the mound or monument at Sarnath, dedicated to the preservation of some Bauddha relics*.

Shortly after this date Benares was wrested from the Gour kings and subjected to the princes of Kanouj. This was the achievement of the third of the race, CHANDRA DEVA, who reigned from 1072 to 1090. It remained in their possession rather more than a century, or till the defeat and death of JAYADEVA.

It is quite certain that MOOHUMMUD GHORY, towards the close of the twelfth century of the Christian era, detached his general KOOTUB-OOD-DEEN against "*the countries* of Kanouj and Benares;" and as a fact is staled highly creditable to the state of the arts at that early period, we may be excused for extracting the paragraph from Colonel STEWART'S translation.

"KOOTUB-OOD-DEEN totally defeated JYCHUND, the Raja of Benares, who fell in the heat of the battle; the number of slain was so great, that for a long "time the body of the Prince could not be found, but was at length recognized *by his artificial teeth, which were fixed with wedges of gold.*

---

* The inscription whence this information was obtained was dug up on the spot, along with some images, gold ornaments, urns, and a few bones, in 1798. It is described in the *Asiatic Researches,* vol. v., and alluded to frequently by Colonel Wilford, who conjectures that the Sarnath monument was partially destroyed by the Moosulmans just after its erection [Sumbut 1083, or A.D. 1027], for the *centres* over which the arches were turned seem never to have been removed.

"After this victory the Sultan himself proceeded to the city of Benares, and demolished nearly one thousand Hindoo temples. Among the spoil taken was a white Elephant, which he presented to Kootub as a proof of "special favor."

This account supposes the battle to have been fought at some distance from the town, and does not advert to the fort, which, according to the other authorities, held out for a considerable time. The lines of circumvallation thrown up by the Moosulman army are very conspicuous to this day; and the site of the old fort shews every where, by the debris of bricks and stones, that it was once covered with houses and temples. It is possible that its demolition had taken place prior to Kootub's invasion,—but it is vain to speculate on the events of the dark and middle ages of India.

From this period we find no allusion to Benares, except as a station of Baber's encampment, with similar occasional cursory notices down to the time of Akber. Its existence as an independent principality and capital had ceased, and it merged into a mere town of the Allahabad or of the Oudh Soubab, under the Mahommedan Empire.

Jounpoor, Allahabad, Chunar, and Rohtasgurh, were the scenes of the struggles and revolutions of Humayoon's reign. The Holy City itself enjoyed comparative tranquillity during the early periods of the Moghul power. Nevertheless, according to the traditions of the *Gungapootras,* or "Sons of the Ganges,"—men whose ancestors have resided on the spot from time immemorial in hereditary attendance upon pilgrims,—the principal place of *teerut'h,* near *Munikurnika Ghát,* must long have continued surrounded by jungul. They even now point out trees built into the walls of houses, as veterans of the original forest. Many of the title deeds of houses in the same neighbourhood date from the first " clearing of the land ;" and Toolsee Das, the celebrated author of the popular version of the

Rámáyana, lived in the sixteenth century (A. D. 1574) "on the skirts of the forest," near the present temple of BHYRONAT'H. There were always, doubtless, habitations and places of worship in abundance, but the rapid increase of the present city, the restoration of its temples, and the embellishment of its *gháts,* mast be dated from the period of the Marhatta ascendancy, when the influence of religion once more drew tribute from the Hindoo Princes of Central India, for the endowment of *Mut'hs* or monastic establishments; and when the place began to benefit by the incomes of court pundits and spiritual ministers, who were glad to spend the evening of their lives in the exercise of religious rites, or in the studious repose of the Holy City.

No building in the town, now standing, can be traced to a higher antiquity than the time of MAN SINGH, who was Raja of Jypoor in the reign of AKBER. Both the temple and observatory, described by TAVERNIER, were erected by him. The astronomical instruments were not added until the time of JY SINGH, A. D. 1680, more than a century later. As the edifices of the city were then exclusively Hindee, built probably by masons from the west, and from genuine ancient plans, these early specimens of architecture are entirely free from the admixture of the Moorish style, which has since been very prevalent.

The bigotry of AURUNGZEBE did not allow many vestiges of this more ancient style to remain. In 1660, for some trifling resistance to the imposition of a capitation tax, he took occasion to demolish the principal Shiwalas, and constructed *Musjids* or mosques with the same materials and upon the same foundations, leaving portions of the ancient walls exposed here and there, as evidences of the indignity to which the Hindoo religion had been subjected.

From this time Benares remained included in the division of the Empire subject to the Nuwab of Oudh, until the reign of MOOHUMMUD SHAH, A.D. 1730, when the Zemindar of the provice, MUNSA RÁM, obtained a *sunud* of Raja in favor of his son BULWUNT SINGH, together with the prerogatives of a mint and courts of justice.

The new Rája still continued to pay the greater part of his revenues to Oudh, until the province was ceded by the Nuwab SHUJA-OOD-DOULUH to the Company in 1773.

The geographical position of Benares was determined by REUBEN BURROW, who places the *Man Mundil,* or Observatory, in lat. 25° 18'36" N. and long. 82° 59'45" E. More recent observations make the latitude 3 seconds and the longitude about two miles less; but the extent of error is, in the latter respect, still uncertain. The distance from Calcutta by the direct road is 420 miles: by water it may be 600 miles. A dak traveller reaches his destination in five days, whereas the journey by water generally employs two months.

The dimensions of the town have been much exaggerated. HAMILTON and other English authors call it six miles in length and four in breadth; whereas, in reality, the measured length along the banks of the river, by survey, is barely three miles, and the average depth does not exceed one mile. Still, from the extreme density of the buildings, and the small space allotted to the streets, it would not be fair to estimate the magnitude from the area only as compared with that of other towns.

Equally erroneous have been the calculations and estimates of the population of Benares, although given on the authority of official records and investigations.

In the year 1803 a census was made by the native Kotwál, under the orders of Mr. DEANE, the city magistrate, which has been published by Lord VALENTIA:—this report states, that there were about 30,000 houses and 600,000 inhabitants; but a very little examination of the data upon which the latter assumption is made, will prove its utter fallacy; for the average of inmates to a house in India has no where else been reckoned at more than five or six, whereas the Kotwál assumed so high an average rate as twenty; and, for a house of six stories, the extravagant estimate of 150 persons!

In the years 1828-29 the designer of these Views undertook to make, unofficially, a revision of the census; and succeeded in completing an entire register of the houses, and proprietors, their names, families, and professions, in the city itself, and in the European station of Secrole and the villages in the immediate vicinity. The results are published at length in the seven-teenth volume of the *Asiatic Researches,* from which the following summary is extracted:

	In the City	*In Secrole* (Sikrour) *and the vicinity.*	
Number of Inhabitants,.........................	1,81,482	11,876	in Native houses.
		7,092	in European houses, including cantonments.
Number of houses or *Chouks*,.............	30,205	2,754	Native houses.
		114	European estates.
Muhullas, as classified in the census,	369	21	
Pukka houses, (of brick or stone,)........	11,325	73	from 1 to 7 stories in height.
Kucha-pukka houses, (mixed,).............	2,328	88	
Kucha houses, (of mud,)......................	16,552	2,639	
Ruins of houses, or blank spaces in streets,..	1,498	72	
Gardens,...	174	114	
Shiwalas or Hindoo temples,................	1,000	7	
Musjids or Moosulman mosques,.........	333	5	
Proportion of Proprietors to Lodgers in seventeen *Muhullas* re-examined, and in the villages,....................................	4,310 to 4,504	7,753 to 1,684	
Proportion of males and females,......... men,..................	3,424	3,354	
women,.............	3,564	3,151	
boys,..................	1,085	1,698	
girls,..................	7 41	1,234	
Proportion of adults to children,..........	4 to 1	2¼ to 1	
Average ratio of inhabitants per *chouk*,	6	6	
Ditto for *pukka* houses in the city,......	7		
Ditto for *kucha* houses ditto,..............	4½		

By way of ensuring accuracy, seventeen *muhullas* were carefully re-examined after the lapse of more than a year, when the numbers were found proportionate to the original census as 8814 to 8932, and most of the discrepancies could be traced to the removal of lodgers, &c.

A minute catalogue was made, at the same time, of the various castes and trades; but as the lists were framed from the information of the *choudrees* or principal men of each sect, who are accustomed to summon their fraternity on occasions of feasts, almsgivings, &c. the same decree of accuracy can not be expected in such an estimate. The following are the results :

	HINDOOS			*NUMBER*	
Brahmans,	*Mahárâshtr*,	11	denominations,	11,311	
	Nágar,	7	ditto,	1,231	
	Mór,	11	ditto,	567	
	Udích,	8	ditto,	1,146	
	Méwáree,	7	ditto,	430	
	Khéréwál,	20	ditto,	2,068	
	Kanya-kubj,	4	ditto,	6,602	
	Gaur,	10	ditto,	1,000	
	Bengálee,	1	ditto,	3,000	
	Gungápootr,	1	ditto,	1,000	
	27 minor sects,			3,026	31,381
Kshétrees,	*Rajpoots*,	2	ditto,	6,200	
	Bhooihar,	1	ditto,	5,000	
	Khetree,	6	ditto,	3,092	
	Baisyas, or Bunyas,	22	ditto,	8,300	
Soodras, including sixty-nine professions,				60,302	
Hindoo Fuqeers, Ramanundees, Sanyasees, Dundees, &c.				7,171	90,065
			Total Hindoo population,		1,21,446
	MUSULMANS				
Raees, or Gentry,				10,000	
Forty-four professions or trades,				20,048	
Fuqeers and Chundáls,				1,200	31,248
					1,52,694
			Add for children and unavoidable omissions,		26,387
			Population as by the *muhulla* census,		1,79,081

By this estimate it would appear that the Musulmans amount to one-fifth of the whole population, which is a large proportion for a Hindoo town; but it may be remarked, that many populous *muhullas* of the suburbs are almost exclusively occupied by weavers who are Mahomeduns.

Among the Hindoos, not less than 20,000 of the Brahmuns, live upon charity, or are supported by endowments in the numerous religious houses and *Mut'hs* of the city. The class of merchants is also very numerous, and comprises many of the richest capitalists of India. The trade in the produce of the district is considerable, comprehending sugar, saltpetre, indigo, opium, and embroidered cloths; besides which, the city has advantages in its position on the great river, making it jointly with Mirzapoor the depot for the commerce of the *Dukhun* and interior of Hindoostan.

Religion, however, may be regarded as the paramount source of supply, —the staple article of commerce through which the Holy City flourishes and is enriched. There need be no fear of this trade declining, so long as the pious have faith in the efficacy of a pilgrimage to *Káshi,* and in the purifying virtues of the Ganges there,—nor while they deem admittance into SHIVA'S Heaven to be secured to them if they die within the limits of the *Punch-kosee* (five koss) circle about the town. Upon great occasions, such as eclipses of the sun or moon, or favorable conjunctions of the planets, incredible multitudes flock in from all quarters to bathe at the consecrated *gháts* of the sacred river: upon one occasion of this sort there were actually counted more than 50,000 persons, bound to the city by its different roads of approach; and frequently the congregation from without must exceed double that number, independently of the resident population.

The visitants from the environs on such occasions disperse as soon as the ceremony is over; but to those who desire to make a complete pilgrimage, a stay of longer duration is necessary; for the *nugur prudukshina,* or circuit of the temples, involves a visit to all the thousand *Shiwalas,* at each of which there are rites to be performed, with prayers and perambulations, which a stout pedestrian would scarcely accomplish in less than a week. Hence has originated a proverbial saying, in summing up the prominent features of worship at Benares, Allahabad, and Gya.

"Káshi hunté,
Pryag mundé,
Gya dundé;"

which may nearly be expressed in English thus :—

At Káshi "keep moving," walk and pray;
At Pryag *shave,*—at Gya *pay!*

The custom of shaving at Pryag arises from the notion, that every hair thrown into the confluence of the Jumna and Ganges purchases the devotee an age of bliss hereafter. The third allusion is aimed at the extortions of the priests, called *Gyalees,* who go seeking dupes over India, whom they persuade to undertake the pilgrimage, and fleece to the last rupee. There is no Government tax on pilgrims at Benares as at the other two places; but immense sums are voluntarily squandered by visitors of rank, in largesses to the Brahmuns, or in the endowment of temples. Many foreign Hindoo Princes entertain delegates or agents at *Káshi,* to perform for their benefit the requisite sacrifices and oblations, and to act as almoners in the daily or periodical distribution of money and grain.

The schools and hallowed retirements of the Benares Pundits are sought after as the fountain-heads of Brahminical learning, and are consequently filled with pupils : but from a prevailing idea that the receiving of remuneration would destroy the merit of teaching the *Vedas,* the Pundits, in most cases, accept of nothing from their scholars, trusting to donations and stipends from Rajas and men of rank. In the present day, encouragement from such quarters is becoming more and more precarious, and Sanskrit learning is consequently on the decline; while the great success of the new colleges in Calcutta, in which the study of European literature is united with that of India, will tend further to eclipse the *alma mater* of rigid Hindooism.

A Sanskrit College was instituted at Benares in 1801, when Mr. DEANE was judge and magistrate. It was maintained out of the public resoures of the province, but remained inefficient for purposes of instruction until within the last few years. It now professedly educates young men to till the important office of pundits to the civil courts, and the study of English has recently been introduced.

There are several missionary day-schools lately established; one of them was richly endowed by a Bengalee Baboo, JYNARAYUN GHOSAL, whose son, KALEESHUNKUR, also, founded an infirmary for the blind, for which benevolent act he received the title of Raja from the Government.

Of the Observatory, Minarets, *Shiwalas,* and other principal edifices, we shall have to speak hereafter, as they are represented in succession in the course of the work. There are, however, it will be remarked, few public offices or institutions, such as would figure in the drawings of other countries as prominent objects for representation. The Courts of Justice, the Treasury, the Mint*, and the Jails, are situated among the European residences at Secrole, and are plain modern structures of brick and mortar. On the other hand, the building material used in the *gháts* and temples is a fine compact sandstone, quarried in the lulls behind Chunar and Mirzapoor, which yield, from this source, an annual revenue to Government of 60,000 Rupees.

---

* The Mint has been since abolished; the premises which it occupied are now the property of the Raja. [1833.]

The stone is frequently coloured red, to imitate the soft sandstone of Agra and Bindrabun, but the white variety is the hardest and most durable. The sharpness and delicacy of the carving on many of the temples is deservedly admired; one of the finest specimens of the skill of the masons in this respect is to be found on the opposite side of the river, in an unfinished *Shiwala* at Ramnugur, of which the whole exterior is covered with minute models of temples and idolatrous images. It was erected by CHYT SINGH, the Raja displaced by Mr. HASTINGS.

When first built, it is customary with the natives to paint their temples and houses with distemper or oil colours; and during the *Diwálee,* in October, the festival which closes the mercantile year, the exterior is always cleaned, and mud walls are repaired and white-washed at the same season. The credit of a merchant who failed to illuminate and make smart his dwelling at this festival, would be very injuriously affected. Indeed the proverbial expression for bankruptcy is, that " such a man's *Diwálee* is extinguished."

The representation of figures on the house-walls is not quite so common at Benares as at Bindrabun and Hurdwar; but it is, nevertheless, frequent. The paintings represent processions and feats of arms, and to European taste are far from ornamental; but they are quite decorous.

The obligation common to all Hindoos, of making daily ablutions in the Ganges, has naturally attracted the chief expenditure towards the *ghàts,* which are handsome and commodious. For two miles the line of stone terraces and steps is uninterrupted; and as the space becomes filled, fresh works are protruded into the river, to the inconvenience of those first laid; so much so, as to be a source of continual disputes.

Notwithstanding the care taken to lay the foundations as deep under water as possible, which is effected at great expense with coffer dams, the river has begun to encroach on the upper end of the *ghâts;* and unless measures are taken to arrest the progress of the mischief, it may produce incalculable injury. The depth of water in front of the town, in the dry season, is more than 50 feet, and the freshes of September add 42 feet to this level. The breadth of the Ganges is 600 yards at low water, and a little more than half a mile in the rains. This splendid stream forms a bay, indenting the front of the town, so as to display its picturesque beauties to great advantage. Indeed there are few objects more lively and exhilarating than the scene from the edge of the opposite sands, on a fine afternoon, under the clear sky of January. The music and bells of a hundred temples strike the ear with magic melody from the distance, amidst the buzz of human voices; and every now and then the flapping of the pigeons' wings is heard as they rise from their crates on the house tops, or whirl in close phalanx round the minarets, or alight with prisoners from a neighbour's flock. At the same time the eye rests on the vivid colours of the different groups of male and female bathers, with their sparkling brass water-vessels, or follows the bulls as they wander in the crowds in proud exercise of the rights of citizenship, munching the chaplets of flowers liberally presented to them. Then, as night steals on, the scene changes, and the twinkling of lamps along the water's edge, and the funeral fires, and white curling smoke, and the stone buildings lit up by the moon, present features of variety and blended images of animation, which it is out of the artist's power to embody. He may give in detail the field upon which these scenes of life are enacted, but the spectator's imagination must supply the rest. Let it be borne in mind, that upon the *ghâts* are passed the busiest and happiest hours of every Hindoo's day:—Bathing, dressing, praying, preaching, lounging, gossiping, or sleeping, there will he be found. Escaping from the dirty, unwholesome and confined streets, it is a luxury for him to sit upon the open steps and taste the fresh air of the river; so that on the *ghâts* are concentrated the pastimes of the idler, the duties of the devout, and much of the necessary intercourse of business.

In no city of the world is the population invited to a single street or place of recreation by so many attractions, and the inhabitants of Benares are justly proud of the beauty and spaciousness of the accommodation provided for them at the river's side. A Native proverb sums up the attractions of *Káshi* in the three words: "*Ranr, Sanr, our Seerhee;*" which may be aptly translated, "Belles, Bulls, and Broad Stairs!"

VIEW FROM UGNESWUR GHAT

This sketch was taken before the river had subsided to its winter level, so that only the upper half of the steps of the *Ghat* is visible. Boats are compelled, at this season, to navigate on the opposite shore, in order to avoid coming in contact with the sunken piers and *murhees* (small temples) of stone.

The minarets of the *Madhoray Musjid* are seen towering aloft from behind a massive stone house, nominally belonging to the Jypoor Raja, but tenanted by a family of Brahmuns or *Poojarees.* The contiguous bastion has lately been purchased by the Ex-Peshwa Bajee Rao, with the intention of erecting a handsome *ghat* and residence thereon*.

About the centre of the drawing stands *Ram ghat,* above which is seen a *Byt'huk* or shaded terrace, where Sudanund Byas, a celebrated preacher, used to lecture to large congregations on the *Vedanta* theology. He is now grown old and very feeble, and ekes out a miserable existence on a daily allowance of one *chitak* of milk.

The white conical spire with gilded *Kulsa,* belongs to the *Jyn Mundil* of Koosula Juttee,—the same of which Bishop Heber gives a minute description. The Bishop has, however, fallen into some inaccuracies in treating of the nature of the *Jyn*

* Since the first edition of these views was published this edifice had been completed, and the present sketch no longer pourtrays Benares *as it is,* but *as it was* in the years 1820-25.

worship. Amongst other things he says, "Their god is called PURNAVESUR;" whereas it is well known to be a fundamental doctrine of the *Jyn* faith, that there is no presiding Deity, but that nature or necessity governs all things. PARISNATH, (the name evidently intended,) is only one of the twenty-four deified sages, or incarnations, to whom the *Jyns* pay reverence, and whose images in black and white marble are set up in niches of the JUTTEE's apartments.

VIEW FROM UGNESWUR GHAT, BENARES

VIEW WESTWARD FROM GHOOSLA GHAT

A cloudless sky, with hard lights and shades, although not the best calculated to please the eye, is very characteristic of the glare and burning atmosphere of Hindoostan. The lanthorns suspended from bamboos, indicative of the *Dipadanu* ceremony in honor of ANANTA, an incarnation of VISHNU, prove the time of this view to be October; and it will be seen that the accumulation of the sand of the rainy season has not been cleared away from the *ghats*.

The canopied Portico and Temple were built by GUHNA BAEE, a Marhatta lady, in honor of the Goddess SHUNKUTA DEBEE :— there is a respectable attendance at the daily lectures at this shrine.

On the right is the house of PUNDITAYUN, the widow of BISUMBHUR Pundit, a Vukeel or Envoy of Nagpoor, who obtained a valuable estate in the Benares district from the bounty of Mr. HASTINGS. The ladies' apartments are screened with close Venetian blinds. A new *ghat* has lately been constructed in front of this house by the nephews of PUNDITAYUN*.

* Beyond the projecting portico, but concealed from view, another magnificent *ghat* has lately been constructed at the expence of the dowager-regent of *Gwalior;* in fact, these improvements are of such constant growth, that the aspect of the city will be different to every successive visitor.

Further on are situated the rich *Dewuls* on *Munikurnika Ghat;* and on the river's edge are seen one or two *Murhees*—chambers into which the sick are removed when at the point of death, that their sins, to the last moment of existence, may be washed away by the holy stream.

VIEW WESTWARD FROM GHOOSLA GHAT, BENARES

Drawn on Stone by J.W. Giles from a Sketch by James Prinsep Esqr. Printed by C. Hullmandel

MADHORAY GHAT AND THE MINARETS

The *Madhoray Musjid* (Mosque) was erected by AURUNGZEBE on the site and with the materials of the Temple of BIND'H MAD'HO, or VISHNOO, which is described by TAVERNIER as having occupied the whole space of ground from *Punchgunga* to *Ram Ghát,* including within its walls the Temples of RAM, and MUNGULA GOUREE, and numerous houses of the priesthood. The imperial zealot, not satisfied with triumphing over the religion of the Hindoos, chose a method of perpetuating the insult most offensive to their habits and feelings, by carrying his minarets to such a height as to overlook the privacy of their houses, the upper apartments and terraced roofs of which are always tenanted by the females of the family. The Mosque has little architectural beauty to boast of, but the *Minars* hare been deservedly admired for their simplicity and boldness of execution. They are only 8¼; feet in diameter at the base, diminishing to 7½ feet at the top, while they have an altitude of 147 feet 2 inches, from the *Suhun* or terraced-floor of the *Musjid* to the *Kulsa* or pinnacle. The terrace is elevated about 80 feet above the river at low water.

At the time of drawing the sketch, the *Musjid* and *Minars* were under repair,—a hazardous undertaking, as regarded the latter, for they were both found to incline outwards 15 inches from the perpendicular. One of them was struck by lightning the very day the scaffolding was removed, but it escaped with the displacement of a stone in the upper cornice or *ch'huja.*

In the course of the last ten years, four or five instances have occurred of men throwing themselves from the top of the southern Minaret. One of them was a man who had gambled away his money and his wife during the *Diwalee:*—another a sailor, who, probably deceived by the height, thought the river within his reach; he fell upon the roof of the house contiguous to the terrace in the sketch, and was killed on the spot:—but a remarkable instance is on record of a Fakeer having once performed the same feat without suffering material injury; he broke through the tiles and mat work of the roof, which tore the flesh from his sides, but he alighted on the floor beneath, with every bone safe: such an escape was deemed miraculous, and crowds attended to reward and minister to one so favoured by heaven. To complete their wonder, the Fakeer disappeared immediately on recovering from his bruises, and sundry solid moveables of his host vanished with him.

MADHORAY GHAT & THE MINARETS AT BENARES

Drawn on Stone by L. Haghe, from a Drawing
by James Prinsep Esqr. Printed by C. Hullmandel

A PREACHER EXPOUNDING THE POORANS IN THE UNNA-POORNA TEMPLE

In many of the customs of Eastern nations we recognize the applicability of Biblical expressions: here we have a Priest "sitting in the corner of the temple teaching the people;" not performing a stated stipendiary duty, but devoting his life to the holy office, and trusting to the voluntary donations of his hearers in food or money, for his daily maintenance.

His *Sing'hásun* serves alternately as a bed, a table, and a pulpit. When a sufficient congregation assembles, (which, by the way, generally comprises a majority of elderly matrons,) the Priest commences his exposition by first chanting the text in Sanskrit from detached leaves of the Sacred *Potee;* he then translates it, and finishes with an appropriate exhortation.

The architecture of the Unna-Poorna Temple is a sample of the mixed style now prevalent: it was built about 60 years ago, and yields a tolerable income to the *Punda,* or lay proprietor.

Unna-Poorna is the name of the consort of Shiva, typified as the Goddess of Plenty; from similarity of her name and attributes, it has been suggested that she is identical with the Anna Perenna of Roman mythology.

A PREACHER EXPOUNDING THE POORANS

In the Temple of Unna-Poorna, Benares Drawn on Stone by L. Haghe from a Drawing by James Prinsep Esqr.

OLD TEMPLE OP VISHVESHVUR

This view is taken from the South-west corner of what is now the *Jumma Musjid* or principal mosque of the city. The dome and minaret surmounting the Hindoo walls are the work of AURUNGZEBE, and the tombs are of the same date.

Antiquarians will he well pleased that the Moosulmans, in their zeal for the triumph of their own religion, discovered a method of converting the original structure into a capacious *Musjid,* without destroying above one half of its walls; so that not only the ground plan, but the entire architectural elevation, may still be traced out. A specimen of the order has been lithographed in the frontispiece, to shew the proportions of the different mouldings.

Part of one of the Hindoo domes also remains: it is not formed on the principle of the arch, but by successive protrusion of the courses of stone, and by cutting off the angles laterally, so as to change the square into a polygon, and thence gradually into a circle; the under edges of the courses are neatly worked up into rosettes and pannels, and present a not inelegant appearance.

The *Lingum* of the original temple of VISHVESHVUR was looked upon as the genuine type of MAHADEO or SHIVA, which fell from heaven upon this spot, and was converted into stone. When the Moosulmans set about their work of destruction, it is asserted, the indignant image leaped of its own accord into the

Gyan Bapee (well of knowledge) hard by, where it still remains. The well has since been considered to be the centre of the *Untrigrihee Jatra,* or Holy Circuit, although a modern *Shiwala,* erected near the spot, pretends to have reinstated the genuine *Lingum,* and fashion is rapidly acquiescing in the arrangement.

Two cases of self-immolation have lately occurred in this temple: the victims cut their throats so that the blood might fall over the image; but the people seemed to regard the act with disgust, and the Brahmuns must be acquitted of having instigated either suicide.

VISHVESHVUR, "Lord of the Universe," is one of the most exalted titles of SHIVA; and his connection with Benares is quaintly depicted in the following sentiment from the *Poorans:* "The *Vedas* and *shastras* all testify that VISVESHVUR is the first of *Devas, Kashee* the first of cities, *Gunga* the first of rivers, and CHARITY THE FIRST OF VIRTUES !"

TEMPLE OF VISHVESHVUR, BENARES

Drawn on Stone from a Sketch by James Prinsep Esqr.

BALCONY AT THE MAN MUNDIR

This specimen of architectural effect can with difficulty be ascribed to so recent a period as the age of Raja MAN SINGH, from whom this Observatory derives its name and existence; for the stone is quite worn away in many places by the weather. It may have belonged to a more ancient building before being set up in its present position by that Chief; but whether executed or borrowed by him, it bears away the palm of antiquity in the town, and is a chef d'œuvre of its kind. It will be remarked, how gradually and skilfully the projection is augmented upwards, so as not to convey the slightest idea of instability : the rule of augmenting the ornamental work with the height, is strictly in accordance with European notions of good taste.

We shall have occasion to speak of the *Man Mundir* itself, when we present a general view of its exterior elevation. The reader will, however, find an elaborate description of the astronomical instruments within the walls of this building, published by Sir ROBERT BARKER, in the Philosophical Transactions of 1775; there is also a pleasing account of a visit made to the place by TAVERNIER, while the young princes of the Jypoor state were studying under the astronomical pundits there.

OLD PROJECTING BALCONY AT THE MAN MUNDIR OR OBSERVATORY, BENARES

Drawn on Stone by C. Hullmandel from a Sketch by James Prinsep Esqr. Printed by C. Hullmandel

HINDOO NACH GIRLS

Without the aid of colour it is scarcely possible to characterise properly the drapery of the damsels who are delineated from the life in this sketch. Their trowsers are of coloured silk:—the full petticoat of striped muslim, with silver or gold embroidery; and the *do-putta* or folded scarf is of stiff crape, with a border of silver brocade.

Too much has been written and said on the subject of the Indian *Nách,* to render any description here necessary. It were a pity to detract from the general illusion that prevails regarding the fairy forms and melodious voices which are wont to breathe seductive raptures amid the exhilarating gambols of the *Hoolee* festival! If, however, beauty and high vocal skill are comparatively rare, the witching influence of the arts and graces of these women is as much acknowledged and as *powerful* as ever. Examples are not wanting of large accumulations of wealth from the successful exercise of the skill and accomplishments of the profession: some of the best houses, and the handsomest temples of the city, have been erected by ladies of dancing notoriety. Their training commences in infancy: the girls being bought as children, are adopted into a partnership or *taefa,* to which their profits belong as a common stock: each rising in turn to the management of the general fund, as she acquires the right by seniority. In order to be freed from the shackles of this partnership, a sum of money to *cover the expense* of board and education, and to compensate the loss of advantage from the acquired talent, must be made good to the association. They are parted with most unwillingly, and there is a reciprocity of affection between the members of each set, which makes them seldom wish to dissolve the tie for ever.

According to the census taken in 1827, there were 264 Hindooee and 500 Moosulmanee professional *Nách* girls in the town; not a very large proportion to the population. There were however four times the number of *khanehgee-kusbees,* who do not profess the accomplishments of singing and dancing.

ULEE BUNDEE

Hindoo Nâch Girl Drawn on Stone by W. Sharp from an original Sketch by James Prinsep Esqr. Printed by C. Hullmandel

A MORNING CONCERT

The instruments represented in this sketch are the *Surinda,* or violin; the *Choutara,* or four-wired guitar; the *Dara,* a kind of tambourine; and the *Surod :* the last is the leading instrument, and is sounded with a plectrum, like other native guitars. The *Surinda* plays in unison with it, while the *Choutara* forms a kind of bass accompaniment, or rather performs the same office as the drone among wind instruments. The men's voices occasionally chime in with the air, and again leave room for some ad libitum movements of the chief performer, who then exerts all his energy in rapid empassioned execution, jerking and tinkling the strings, and wagging his head with every intonation, until his enraptured audience applaud him with the flattering "*wah wah! sha-bash, sha-bash!*"

None of the stringed instruments in use among the natives have either the power of the violin or the mellowness of the guitar: they resemble more in sound the hurdy-gurdy and the mandoline; yet, in skilful hands, they are capable of much expression; and the soft melancholy cadence of Hindoostanee music accords very agreeably with the languid influence of an oriental climate.

Surinda Choutara Dara Surod

A MORNING CONCERT

Drawn on Stone by W. Sharp from an original Sketch by James Prinsep Esqr. Printed by C. Hullmandel

T'HUT'HEREE BAZAR

Some apology may be necessary for introducing so imperfect a sketch into our series: it will suffice, however, to explain the general features of a Benares Street, confined, crooked, and so narrow, "that even narrow seems a term too wide !"

The *Silpa-Shastra* (a compendium of architectural ordinances in the Hindoo scriptures) prescribes that there should be no deviation from the right angle in the ground plan of a duelling, and that the four sides should face the cardinal points of the compass as nearly as possible. When, therefore, a street takes an oblique direction, which is indispensable, where cities are built on rivers deviating from their right line, it encounters a succession of projecting corners on either side, leaving spaces to be filled up with *chubootras,* or raised seats. These are let out as stalls to venders of trinkets, toys, and confectionery.

The house in front is built in Bengalee taste, with a barbarous admixture of European architecture.

The street receives its name from the braziers or makers of *lotas* and other brass vessels, who during the day occupy the lower apartments of the houses facing the street as *dookans* or shops. Even the largest houses are constructed in this manner; and the shops, shut off by a dead wall from the inner apartments, at once offer protection and privacy to the interior court or *chouk.*

T'HUT'HEREE BAZAR

(The widest Street in Benares)

BENARES FROM THE MUNDAKINEE TULAO

The *Mundakinee* forms one of a series of *j'heels* or ponds, which intersect the town in a line nearly parallel to the river, and seem to have been formerly a back channel for the superfluous floods of the Ganges in the rainy season. By the construction of a tunnel drain under the town at Trilochun, these *Tulaos* were laid dry a few years ago, and the site of one of them is now converted into a grain market. The *Mundakinee* being stocked with turtles, which were looked upon with veneration, and regularly fed by the Hindoos, a merchant volunteered to pay two annas a head for all that should be *removed* alive into the river upon the draining of the tank. The number thus caught and transplanted exceeded 1500, many of them weighing from two to three maunds, that is, upwards of two hundred pounds.

The Sanskrit College occupies a disagreeable position on the right of the *Tulao,* close to the mouth of the main sewer. The mound to the left, with a cottage upon it, belongs to an order of religious mendicants, termed *Kunp'hutta* (slit-eared) Jogees, who wear large crystal or agate circular discs, fitted through their ears as ear-rings. They do duty as ministers in rotation at the temple of BHYRONATH, who is an attendant, or a form of, SHIVA, and is exhibited riding upon a dog, and holding in his hands a horn and a drum. It is his province to grind between millstones those who violate the laws of the *Shastras* during their residence in *Kashee.*

BENARES FROM THE MUNDAKINEE TULAO
Drawn on Stone by J.D. Harding from a Sketch by James Prinsep Esqr. Printed by C. Hullmandel

VIEW FROM PUNCHGUNGA GHAT

In the corner of a cul-de-sac to the north-west of the minarets is a small *p'hatuk,* or gate, opening upon a steep flight of steps, at the foot of which extends the ghat of *Punchgunga* (the five rivers), where a considerable fair is held during the month of *Kartik* (Oct. Nov.), and where it is prescribed to bathe every morning before sun-rise, throughout the same month.

The author of the *Kashi-khund* is driven to the never-failing resources of mythological legend, or his own equally prolific invention, to account for the presence of the five rivers, which are supposed to give such peculiar sanctity to this spot.

A virgin named *D'hooátpápa,* whom BRUHMA pronounces to be more pure than three and a half crore of the holy *teeruths* (places of pilgrimage), having cause of complaint against her admirer *Dhurma,* politely pronounces a malediction upon him, and turns him into the *Dhurma-nada* (river of virtue) : he in revenge converts her into a rock; but her father, *Vedasoor,* in compassion metamorphoses her again into the *Chundrakanta* (moon-stone), which melting in the moon, forms a stream called *D'hootápápa* (cleanser of sin), an appropriate bride for the river of virtue.

The third stream, called *Kirn-nuddee* (brook of rays), was produced from the perspiration of the sun while performing penance, in honor of *Mungulagouree* (a form of *Devi),* on an adjoining ghat. These three, with the *Gunga* and *Suruswutee,* complete the number of the *Punchanada,* to the satisfaction even of the deities themselves, who condescended to bathe on the spot during their residence in *Kashi*.

On the opposite side of the river is just visible the commencement of the road to Calcutta.

VIEW OF THE GANGES

From the Phatuk or Gate at the top of Punchgunga Ghat Drawn on Stone by William Walten from a Sketch by James Prinsep Esqr. Printed by C. Hullmandel

VIEW OF THE CHURN-PADOOKA ON MUNIKURNIKA GHAT

After *Kashi* had been created by the united will of *Iswur* and *Parbutee,* the two incorporated energies of the formless and qualityless *Bruhm,* the active pair determined to give their paradise the benefit of an inhabitant, and *Poorooshotama* (the supreme male, VISHNOO) became manifest. SHIVA gave him instructions how to behave himself, and left him to his own meditations; whereupon as a first exploit, with his *chukra,* or discus, he dug the tank situated to the right and beyond the limits of the accompanying view; and denominated from its origin the *Chukr-pooshkurni.* He then engaged in the usual course of austerity, at the sight of which SHIVA shook his head in astonishment, and one of his earrings fell, whence the name of the ghat, *Munikurnika,* (jewel of the ear :) VISHNOO upon this spot also obtained as a boon from *Mahadeo* the privileges which *Kashi* enjoys, of giving *mookti* or emancipation to all objects, especially those who bestow gifts, erect lingas, and do not commit suicide within the holy precincts.

The *Churn-padooka* (impression of VISHNOO's feet), is said to mark the spot on which he alighted; it is distinguished by the figure of two feet cut in white marble, in the centre of a round slab, probably intended to represent the *chukr* or discus : but as the *churn* is generally thought to be peculiar to Booddha and Jain places of worship, the emblem is probably of modern and spurious introduction where it is here set up. There is another *padooka* near the mouth of the Burna Nala, where also VISHNOO, it is said, in one of his visits

> "Down right into the world's first region threw
> His flight precipitant."

The two temples were built by Ahila Baee; and another Marhatta lady erected and endowed the *Noubut khaneh,* or orchestral pavilion on the right, from which at sun-rise and sun-set, the wild rambling sounds of the *Sunai* (hautboy), and the prolonged drone of the Rambhempoo, with the varying roll of the "Indian drum"—expanding through the amphitheatre of ghats, awakens similar feelings to those felt, in other climes, at the distant chime of village bells, or the swell of a cathedral organ.

BENARES

A Brahmin placing a Garland on the holiest Spot in the sacred City. Drawn on Stone by J.D. Harding from a Sketch by James Prinsep Esqr. Printed by C. Hullmandel

RAJRAJESWUREE GHAT

The facade of this building is a good specimen of the mixed style of Hindoo and Moresque architecture; the former is observable in the lower half of the central compartment, while the projecting stone gallery with its parapet, *tukya mootukka,* and the domed octagonal *booruj* at the two corners, giving relief to the rectangular pavilion in the centre, are seen to be essentially Moorish from the character of the pillar, and scalloped arch *(mehrab).* There ought to have been a flight of steps from the gate-way to the water's edge; but probably the work was suspended, by a quarrel about the boundary line, between the founder Bhuwanee Gir Gosaeen, and his neighbour the proprietor of the Oomrao Gir Pooshta on the right, which is likewise incomplete; for, though both parties have long been dead, when it became an object of the Improvement Committee to carry a drain under the ghat at this place, a violent dispute arose as to which party should have the privilege of paying for it; each expecting thereby to confirm his right to the ground. The groupe depicted in the sketch represents the Committee's Daroga and his myrmidons, settling this knotty point by actual inspection of the premises !

The ghat takes its name from an ancient temple to Debee under the appellation of the *Rajrajeswuree* "queen of queens;" the same is quoted by Colonel Wilford, (upon doubtful authority however,) as the name under which Bhuwanee made her appearance on the banks of the Nile.

**RAJRAJESWUREE GHAT
BENARES**

PROCESSION OF THE TAZEEAS

For ten days in the month of *Mohurrum,* the Moosulmans are seen clad in green and black, their trappings of woe, in commemoration of the martyrdom of HUSUN and HOOSYN, the sons of ULEE, and grandsons of the prophet. Husun was killed in battle on the plain of Kerbela, A. D. 680; his elder brother is supposed to have been poisoned some time after at Medina. The circumstances attending the death of the *Imams* are recited at night in all the musjeeds belonging to the *Shia* sect, which comprehends most of the lower orders in Benares. The piteous tale is chaunted in the current language by people hired, apparently, for their strength of lungs, who work themselves and their audience by decrees into a phrenzy of grief; tearing their hair, beating their breasts, and crying "*Hoosyn, Hoosyn,*" until quite exhausted. It was under such a state of excited zeal, that a congregation at the *Lat'h Imambareh,* in 1805, was urged by some fanatic preacher to overthrow and defile the pillar and images of Hindoo worship at that place; the imprudent feat, however, caused a furious reaction, and might have ended in the extermination of the weaker party throughout the town, but for the judicious intervention of Mr. W. W. Bird, then Magistrate, and the really docile and submissive temper of the Hindoos.

More danger is generally apprehended from the collision of the two sects of the faithful among themselves; an increasing opposition having within these few years been organized by the *Soonees* against the practice of celebrating the Mohurrum within the precincts of the musjids, and of carrying the *tazeea* (a model of the mausoleum at Kerbela containing the tomb of the Imam) in public procession, and giving it regular burial at the conclusion of the festival. At Allahabad, the troops have been drawn out more than once for the preservation of peace. But the custom, though unsupported by authority, has acquired too firm a hold among the populace to be easily relinquished.

The present drawing represents the spot in which the tazeeas are buried at Benares : they were formerly merely thrown into the ditch that is visible on the left hand, until the establish-ment of the burial place by *Shekh Ulee Hujee,* a saint of royal descent, who came hither from Persia in 1750. The place derives its name from a *Durgah* or mausoleum, which he erected in honor of *Fatima* the wife of the prophet, (corrupted into *P'hatman* by the vulgar.) Since his time many have embellished it with monuments and mosques: the garden of the Delhi prince *Juwan Buk'ht* adjoins, containing some handsome tombs, the stone net-work of which is much admired.

Shekh Ulee Hujee is a great favorite with the Hindoos, who are fond of quoting a couplet of his, expressive of a reciprocal attachment on his part:

"*Uz Bunarus nu ruu'um, mabid-i âm ust eenja;*
Hur Brahmun pisr-i Luchmun o Ram ust eenja !"

I love Benares,—peaceful sanctity pervades the place,—
Where every Brahmun boasts descent from RAMA's holy race!

PROCESSION OF THE TAZEEAS

During the Mohurrum at the Phatman a Moosulman Burying Ground, Benares Drawn on Stone by George Barnard from a Sketch by James Prinsep Esqr. Printed by C. Hullmandel

BRUHMA GHAT

THIS ghat is ancient, and of irregular form; it derives its name from a temple of Shiva, under the title of Bruhmeswur, "the lord of Bruhma," or "the *lingum* erected by Bruhma," situated at the top of the stairs.

The circumstance of such an appellation might appear irreconcileable with the rank generally ascribed to the persons of the Hindoo triad, but for the explanation given in the *Kashi-khund,* which states, that when SHIVA, and all the Divinities had been compelled to resign *Kashi* to the earthly virtues of DIVADAS, BRUHMA was one of the first to return in disguise to the sacred city and obtained leave of the king to set up a lingum in honour of SHIVA, on this spot, giving in the usual way his own name, epithetically, to designate and distinguish the linage :—there are numberless lingums, such as Doorgeswur, Rameswur, Hunoomuteswur, Gunesheswur, &c. derivable from a similar origin.

The temple and ghat were repaired (perhaps built) two hundred years ago by the Marhattas, and again recently by the ex-Peshwa Baji Rao. From the number of Marhatta families residing in the neighbourhood, and the comparative privacy of the spot, it is by courtesy set apart as a bathing place for their women; the upper classes among whom are distinguished by the fairness of their complexions, as well as by the variety of colours displayed in their costume.

They resort hither in groupes, with their children and female servants. Their bathing dress consists of a *dhotte* similar to that worn by the men, but longer, and generally of pink, purple, or yellow silk; a close boddice; and a silk scarf over the shoulders. Their wet garments are shifted with dexterity under a large wrapper, which is worn also over the silk dress, in passing through the streets homewards. The brahmun of the ghat is of course a privileged person; he receives a small gratuity for taking care of the clothes and brass or silver water-vessels; he also affixes the *tiluk* (frontal mark), and pronounces the *muntra* or morning benediction upon his spiritual daughters.

BRUHMA GHAT, BENARES

Drawn on Stone by George Barnard from a Sketch by James Prinsep Esqr. Printed by C. Hullmandel

VIEW OF THE MAN MUNDIL

The "house of Man" forms one of the most picturesque objects for the artist's pencil, from the commanding altitude and antiquated irregularity of its front, enhanced by the expanse of never-ending steps at its base, and a back-ground well suited to the effects of light and shadow. Of one of the projecting balconies, a drawing was given in the first series: the rest are in a more dilapidated state, and the lower gallery is much corroded by the alternate action of the atmosphere and the river. The building was converted into an observatory by JYSING, A. D. 1680, and a lively description is given by Tavernier, of the dignity of the establishment, when he visited it: two of the young princes of Jypoor were then pupils there, studying astronomy under skilful pundits : alas ! the change is now so complete, that hardly an astronomer in town can explain the nature or use of the instruments which remain!—and the old woman who acts as cicerone to visitors, confesses, "all she knows is, that what she calls *sooruj* (the sun), we foreigners call *aftáb!*"

The large stone azimuth circle is seen towering above the centre of the building; the principal gnomon is not visible from the river—nor are the mural quadrant and equatorial ring. The rooms nearest to the spectator were the residence of the chief pundit, who had a small equatorial dial on the top of his house, to serve, no doubt, as his private chronometer.

The broken wall beyond is part of the *Meerpooshta,* the foundations of which were undermined by the river a few years ago. Raja Oodutnarayun Singh purchased the ruins for twenty thousand rupees, intending to restore the terrace and ghat on a grander scale; but his zeal has since abated. The groupe in the foreground represents a Marhatta family crossing a ferry.

VIEW OF THE MAN MUNDIL
or Hindoo Observatory, Benares
Drawn on Stone by George Barnard from a Sketch by James Prinsep Esqr. Printed by C. Hullmandel

MUNIKURNIKA GHAT

THIS view is intended principally to exemplify the structure of the ghats on the water's edge. The continuity of the line of steps is interrupted by hundreds of stone piers of various forms, which may be classed under three distinct heads : some are merely intended to give solidity to the masonry, as is shewn in the engraving of Ghoosla ghat: others are built for the accommodation of the *ghateeas* (ghat attendants), and *Gungapootras* (sons of the Ganges), who enjoy hereditary possession of most of the ground between high and low water mark : the third sort consists of *mut'hs* or *murhees* (small temples), erected at the expence of pilgrims and others; they generally have a flat roof to serve still as a *chubootra* for the proprietor or *ghateea* to sit upon, who not unfrequently allows the temple to fall into premature decay, and sells the space again to another pious dupe. As a criterion of the value of such property, it may be mentioned, that when Maharaja Sindeea, in 1829, wished to repair the dilapidated ghat of Beereswur, next adjoining to Munikurnika ghat, he could not obtain the good will of the *Gungapootras* under 15,000 rupees, although they were promised the reconstruction of their *chubootras,* and their right of occupancy was to remain uninfringed.

The octagonal *mut'h* towards the right hand, marks the south corner of Ahulya Baee's ghat: one of the niches outside is embellished with a small white marble figure of this celebrated princess in a sitting posture. She caused the two temples represented in the sketch to be erected, on the site of others, which had been carried away by the river. The same fate seems to threaten the new structures also at no very distant period, as the whole strength of the stream is exerted to undermine them. In the rains the temples are submerged to the cornice; many Hindoos, notwithstanding, are bold enough to swim through an impetuous current, and to dive under the porch and door-way, for the honor of continuing their customary worship in despite of perils and personal inconvenience.

MUNIKURNIKA GHAT, BENARES

from the river

Drawn on Stone by George Barnard from a Sketch by James Prinsep Esqr. Printed by C. Hullmande!

THE THAKOOR-DWAREE

Every family of respectability maintains an establishment for the service of their family religious rites :—a *gooroo* or pundit to give the *muntras,* or benedictions and absolutions, who also serves as a tutor for the children :— a *purohit* or priest to perform the ceremonies of marriage; *sradd'h,* or the worship of manes, &c.;—and a *poojéree,* or under-priest, to go through the ordinary routine of *pooja* to the *Thakoors* [gods] in the sanctuary or *Thakoor-dwaree :* he has to clean their altars, to administer the daily offerings of rice, flowers, and incense; to cook their dinner, and to make their bed ! Each member of the family is expected also to repair, morning and evening, to the sanctuary to offer up his own petitions : and those who do not bathe at the river side, perform their ablutions within the same apartment, a division being made for the purpose. The present sketch was taken in the house of Lala Kashmeree Mul : the whole house is in the same rich style of architecture, but the present proprietors are too poor to keep it in repair. One of the white marble screens, the match to that shewn in the plate, has been sold, along with the marble floor of the bath ! The roof of the chamber is of a dark wood richly embossed. The dimensions of the whole are upon a small scale.

The curiosity of the English reader will naturally expect a list of the paraphernalia of the temple : The altar or shrine upon which they stand is called *Sin'ghasun.* There are a number of small images in silver or brass, of *Bruhma, Doorga, Krishna,*

Rama, Gunesh, Hunooman, &c.: item, several linga of Mahadeo, —at least two *Saligrams* (fossil impressions of the ammonite shell from the Himalaya, supposed to have been left there by VISHNOO when he hid himself under the earth in the form of a snake ;—the fossil shell itself is called *Sesnat'h* (the snake god):—) also a white marble image of *Nundee* the bull: item, of utensils for *pooja;* a large *Shunk'h* or conch shell to be sounded like a horn : a *padma shunkh* (small shell) to pour water over the images : a *Kosha* and *Kooshee,* long copper cup and spoon, and two or three brass plates to serve up the sacrificial repast, and a five-branched candlestick : of musicals;—*ghunta,* a large bell, *kansa*, a gong, *sunai, mridung,* and *kurtal,* hautboy, drum, and cymbals—besides a due supply of rice, flowers, incense, &c. &c.

A THAKOOR-DWAREE

Interior of Lala Kashmeeree Mul's House, Benares Dii Penates and Sacra in the Sanctum Day & Haghe Lithrs to the King 17, Gatest. Drawn on Stone by L. Haghe, from a Sketch by James Prinsep Esqr.

EVE OF AN ECLIPSE OF THE MOON

Conjunctions of the planets, eclipses, and *sankrant,* or the Sun's entrance into the zodiacal signs, are accounted the most auspicious moments for bathing in the Ganges; and the act is so much the more efficacious, if performed at Koorookshetr, Kashi, or other places of *teerut'h* situated on the holy stream.

For two or three days previous to such an event, pilgrims and travelling parties from the country round, frequently even from greater distances, begin to assemble in groupes upon the terraces and balconies of the temples and houses near the river. Every vacant spot is put in requisition and hired out by the square foot: even the khadim of the Minaret-mosque does not scruple, for a *consideration* of about 200 rupees, to throw open the *suhun* or floor of the Musjid for the accommodation of the children of superstition ! Indeed it may be remarked, that on most occasions of festive and multitudinous assemblage, the distinctions of religion give way, and the scene bears more the character of a fair *(méla)* than of a religious meeting : booths, whirligigs pastry cooks, and penny trumpets, are accompaniments as indispensable upon such occasions in India as in more civilized parts of the globe. At the eclipse of the 25th Nov. the crowd was unusually great, and no less than forty lives were lost in the press of bathers at the first glimpse of the moon's obscured visage. Most of the figures in the view were drawn and finished on the spot; for a scene so brilliant, in the delightful weather of November, was too attractive to be quitted while any tiling remained to be seen. Not the least curious spectacle, indeed, was the rapid dispersion of the crowd after the ceremony was over, (for night is the season of travel in India.) so that on the morrow hardly a vestige, remained of the turbulent scene, save where lay the scattered corpses of the unfortunate victims, chiefly women and children, who had been crushed to death by the ruthless multitude of the night.

The smoke on the left hand points out the spot on which the dead are burned, a place dedicated to VISHNOO, as *Julsaeeor* "sleeper upon the waters," and where, many a widow has undergone the severe trial enjoined by her religion, with a constancy to be admired while shuddered at. After-ages will applaud the resolution which has in our time abolished a practice so abhorrent to human nature.

In the crowd are seen a couple of Missionaries distributing tracts with zeal as ardent, and perhaps as unavailing, as that of the poor *Suttees* themselves.

EVE OF AN ECLIPSE OF THE MOON

25th November 1825 Drawn on Stone by L. Haghe, from a Sketch by James Prinsep Esqr.

GHOOSLA GHAT

Ghoosla Ghat unites great solidity with a graceful and appropriate elevation; the double arched door-case in front of the gate has a very rich effect under the strong shadows of mid-day, giving an artificial magnitude to the entrance, in just proportion to the dimensions of the front. The large extent of blank wall *(pooshta),* it must be remembered, is unavoidable, from the height of the bank; the terrace or roof being merely on a level with the street above. There is however, to our ideas, an unnecessary waste of materials in the extreme solidity of these buildings, especially in the superstructure, which instead of being a flanking wall with bastions and counterforts, is entirely solid masonry constructed with rough stones *(dhoka)* and grouting, and faced with flat slabs *(oobwut),* attached firmly to the wall by longitudinal and vertical coping stones *(rasee kadáb* and *furk, hee)* as represented by the faint lines in the drawing. The river rises above the top of the door-way, entering the staircase, and affording a comfortable bath within, where there are convenient recesses on the sides of the steps for the accommodation of bathers.

The temple on the terrace above, is an exquisite specimen of minute sculpture, and well deserves to be visited by the curious in architectural ornament at the expence of mounting the steep ascent. It is dedicated to *Lukshminarayun)* a combination of the names of VISHNU and LUKSHMI his wife, and was built at the beginning of the present century by order of the Raja of Nagpoor.

The service of this temple is kept up with due solemnity, and regular expositions of the *Bhagavat-gita* are made daily after *Pooja,* by the priests of the establishment.

Some indulgence is solicited for this and the other outline engravings given in the present series: they have been executed by a Native, who has much to learn in perspective both aerial and linear; in other respects the plates are creditable enough to the progress of the Arts in Calcutta.

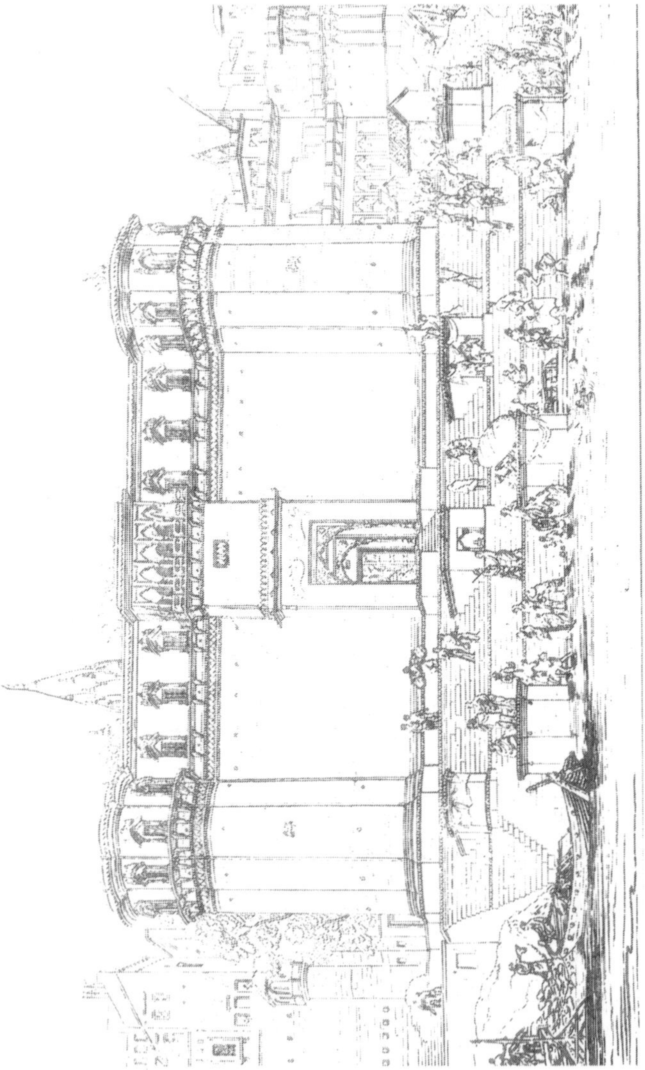

GHOOSLA GHAT, BENARES

Drawn on Stone by Kasheenath Sculps, from a Sketch by James Prinsep Esqr.

SHREEDHUR MOONSHEE'S GHAT and RANA MUHUL

Shreedhur, formerly one of the ministers of the Raj of Nagpoor, retired from office in the year 1812, and obtained permission to reside at Benares. He built a magnificent edifice of stone to the south of Kewulgir ghat, of which the present engraving gives but an imperfect idea. The Moonshee died in 1824, leaving, as his heir, an adopted child of the name of Narayun Rao. The *Rana Muhul,* or Prince's buildings, as it may be rendered in English, was erected by the Rana of Oodypoor, in the seventeenth century, for the accommodation of travellers and pilgrims resorting from his dominions to Benares :—most of the Hindoo princes entertain similar establishments in the town.

After the rainy season, when the river subsides, the ghateeas make up here and there, large images, with the earth accumulated upon the ghats, which they paint in gaudy colours and designate by the general name of *Bhima Sen,* this second of the five sons of *Pandu,* so renowned in the wars of the Mahabharat. Bhima was a giant of prodigious strength, famous for his skill in wielding the *guda,* or spike-headed mace: pooja is offered to his image in the month of Kartik, by those who are very punctilious in the observance of what may be called the saints days of the Hindoo calendar.

The women seated in a row on the margin of the water are engaged in making up little clay images of the *lingam,* which they place beside them, sprinkle with water, milk, flowers, &c. and finally fling into the river, repeating their prayers all the time, with frequent introduction of the words "*Sudasyoo, Visveswur*" and other names of SHIVA. This ceremony is ordained by the Kashi-khund for every forenoon throughout the month of Sawun, after bathing in the Ganges.

SHREEDHUR MOONSHEE'S GHAT AND RANA MUHUL, BENARES

Drawn on Stone by Kasheenath Sculps, from a Sketch by James Prinsep Esqr.

ELEVATION OF A HINDOO TEMPLE

Architecture, like every other branch of the arts among the Hindoos, is an hereditary occupation. The head masons or *Rajmistrees* employed in the construction of temples and edifices of a superior description, have generally in their possession, a number of plans and elevations handed down as heir-looms in their families, along with extracts or detached leaves of the *Silp-Skastra,* which few or none of them in the present day are able to read, and which are in general of so technical a nature as to be but imperfectly understood by the Pundits themselves. These plans, along with a variety of designs for mouldings, scrolls, lattice work, &c. supply materials for all modern buildings of the purer Hindee taste; but many builders have ventured to engraft the Moosulman or Moresque style upon the latter, and, where skilfully combined, the mixture has a very good effect: frequent examples of it have occurred in the foregoing sketches : the present *dewul* (temple) is, however, essentially Hindee.

The *order*, or the proportion of the several parts, is most clearly developed in the central compartment of the elevation, on both sides of which it is continued through a multitude of retiring and salient angles, in accordance with the contour of the ground plan. The elevation may be divided into four parts:

I. The *K'hoora,* hoof, buttress, or basement, whence may probably be derived the word *k'hoorsee,* made use of by native bricklayers for the plinth of a wall.

II. The *Jang'hee,*—leg or thigh: forming what we should call the shaft or trunk of the order.

The upper and lower parts of the *Jang'kee* are frequently richly moulded with several rows of *pucht'hura,* a moulding so called from its five fillets, tiers, or courses *(panch sthula,* Sans.) the two first retiring, the third forming the neck, and the upper two projecting to correspond with those below. The flat wall of the *Jang'hee* is also commonly ornamented with flowers and scrolls, as at the Vishveshwur Shiwala, or covered with minute dewuls, each containing a *deota,* or image, in high relief. The *Jang'hee* is surmounted by a deeply projecting cornice or *ch'huja,* resting upon the *kunt'ha,* or throat of the third *purht'hura.* The principal member of the ch'huja is finished with a torus or *gola,* from which are suspended a row of drops, called *kounlee* or lotus buds : on the upper edge are carved semicircular scallops to match, which are named *thikaree,* (probably *tikaree,* from their resemblance to the *tika* or frontal wafer.)

III. The *Soorra* or spire, (probably a corruption of *choora,* Sanskrit. Gilehrist's dictionary gives *sool* as Hindee for spire, which is most likely the same word, as the r is often converted into an 1.)

The *Soorra* may be subdivided into

1. The *gulla,* or neck, which serves as a kind of pedestal, and is surmounted by the *chhujlee,* a small cornice or gallery; in the centre of this member is introduced a niche for the image of Gunesh; at this stage of the building the architect marks out the *bhuddur,* or diagram, which determines the number and position of the spires.
2. The *soorra* proper, may be either a single spire or a cluster of any number, according to the ground plan laid down by the architect:—the corner edges are sometimes

richly carved, or even pierced through, as in the Vishveshwur temple; the spire is crowned by

3. The *kulsa,* or pinnacle : this word signifies water-jar, which clearly points out its origin, for the same kind of ornament is often seen at the gable ends of tiled roof's, actually made of different earthen water vessels threaded upon an upright stick. The *kulsa* consists of the following members :

   Tirsool—the trident of Mahadeo.

Bal—a stick—the thread on which sugar is crystallized, probably the projecting point of the stick on which the *kulsa* is threaded. This member is sometimes called *kounlee.*

Mutkee—a small hemispherical water-pot; sometimes called *toomba.*

Gngra—a common water-pot.

Kungnee—a rim, ring or bracelet.

Morha—the opening or vent of the *soorra;* covered with the *chupun* or stopper.

Ounra—the myrobalan fruit: a moulding which is turned over or folded upwards.

Hamrekha—the Vaishnava frontal mark—consisting of a horizontal line with three uprights, the two outer curved outwards, the centre straight, it resembles the trident, and in Hindee architecture, forms a common finish to the upper edge of projecting stones.

It is uncertain whether the portico is a necessary appendage to the pyramidal temples; it is now generally added, but it does not unite well; unless where, unlike the present example, the spire of the portico is compressed into a mere cluster of kulsas, when it looks much more symmetrical with the rest of the building.

IV. The *Balundur*—Viranda or portico, probably *bulum-dhur,* supported by staves,— has the same basement and cornice as the temple, but differs in being open and supported by columns; it is generally tetrastyle, having two rows of four columns, which are of an order expressly set apart for the temples.

The *dewulee khumbha,* or temple column, contains the following parts:

1. *Purgaha*—the base :—or a particular moulding on the *choukee* or base.
2. *Dwarpal*—the door-keeper; a figure cut in relief, standing in a niche.
3. *Dewulee*—the type or model of a temple, which seems to be an inverted lotus.
4. *Soluhwans*—the sixteen bamboos or flutes: this compartment is sometimes bevilled off into an octagon, it is crowned by a band scalloped on the under edge, *j'halur*, of which a great variety of patterns is to be seen on the coping stones of wait, plinths, piers, &c.
5. *Ghuntee*—sixteen little bells, corresponding in number with the sides of the shaft under the capital, or
6. *Mutkee*—the water-pot before mentioned, but ornamented with 4 handles or ears, adapting it to the abacus or square slab crowning the pillar, which in the example before us is ornamented with a *choudanee putta* or four studded leaf. Upon the capital immediately rests the *ch'huee*, a member unknown in the Grecian orders,— the word signifies shade or shadow ;—its object is to contract the opening above, and by spreading laterally about one breadth beyond the capital, to give better support to the architrave or *dab*; the angles of the projecting part are cut off into the form of brackets with

different devices, and the moulding on the lower edge of the *dab,* [in this case a *gulta,* or cavetto,] is continued down the sides of the ch'huee.

7. The *Dab* or architrave, containing a small image of GUNESH in a pannel. In the present case, as here is no frieze, the modillions—*keechuk* (small bamboo) or *ghora* (horse or bracket to support a shelf) are inserted into it, for the support of the cornice.

The entablature terminates with another *jhalur,* and the *ch'huja* or cornice of the main temple; above which is continued the range of *puchf'hura* mouldings, surmounted by a spire: there is sometimes substituted for the latter, a kind of pediment of which the apex is rounded off: an example may be seen in the view of Munikurnika Ghat.

PLAN OF THE OLD VISHVESHWUR TEMPLE

Having exceeded our limits in explaining the architectural terms of the last plate, we must dismiss the present with a hare notice. It is intended to explain the native method of protracting a ground-plan *(ch'henkun)* by the method of squares *(ilachee marna)*. The interior diameter of the temple is apparently taken as the modulus for all the other measurements; and has the subdivision into sixteen parts (half only are represented in the engraving) which is common alike to the units of weight, of value, and of area among the Hindoos. In the Vishveshwur Mundir the actual length of the modulus is sixteen *guj,* or about 35 feet. The laying out of the angles *(nagur),* forming the external figure of the plan, is culled the *B'hudra* or diagram, upon which depends the number and conformation of the spires *(chooras)* above; they are all determined by strict rules.

The darkly shaded part shews the figure and foundations of the principal *dewul:* the fainter, those of the outer *dewulees.* The whole must have formed, when complete, a picturesque groupe of nine spires around a central pyramid. The heights diminishing from the centre towards the corners in the proportions of sixteen, eight, and six, as seen by the ground plan.

The principal *lingam* of *Mahadeo* stood in an ornamented reservoir in the centre, having a drain below to carry off the

Ganges water continually poured over it by day and night. *Mundip* signifies vestibule: *Dundpan* and *Dwarpal* are respectively the staff-bearer and door-keeper. The latter situation is held by *Kál Bhyro,* the offspring of SHIVA's rage; the former appointment was conferred upon *Hurikeshu,* a *Yukshu,* or one of the attendants upon the Deity of riches, in reward for his having abandoned the sports of youth to devote himself to ascetic meditation at *Kashi. Tarakeswur* and *Manikeswur* are two inferior lingums of SHIVA.

For the elevation corresponding with this plan, the reader is referred to the plate of the same temple in the First Series.

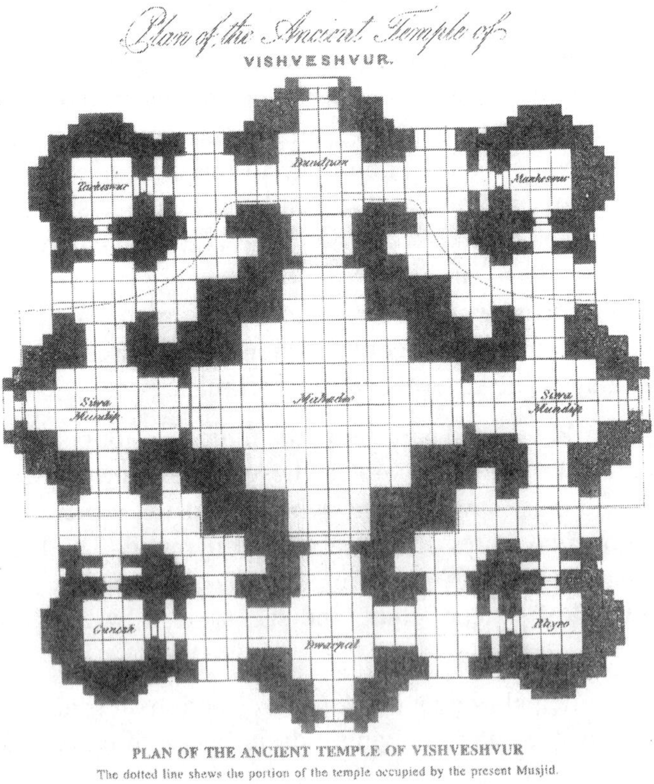

PLAN OF THE ANCIENT TEMPLE OF VISHVESHVUR

The dotted line shews the portion of the temple occupied by the present Musjid.

VIEW OF THE GYAN BAPEE WELL, BENARES

Drawn on Sione by L. Haghe, from Sketch by James Prinsep Esqr.

KUPULDHARA TULAO, BENARES

Drawn on Stone by L. Haghe from Sketch by James Prinsep Esqr.

RAM LEELA MELA

Drawn on Stone by L. Haghe from Sketch by James Prinsep Esqr.

BHURUT MELAO

Drawn on Stone by George Barnard from a Sketch by James Prinsep Esqr. Printed by C. Hullmandel

LAL SHAH'S TOMB AND GHAZIMEEA KE DURGAH BENARES

Drawn on Stone by George Barnard from a Sketch by James Prinsep Esqr. Printed by C. Hullmandel

DUSASWUMEDH GHAT

BENARES

Drawn on Stone by L. Haghe from a Sketch by James Prinsep Esqr. Printed by C. Hullmandel

BOORWA MUNGUL FESTIVAL, AT BENARES

Drawn on Stone by L. Haghe from a Sketch by James Prinsep Esqr. Printed by C. Hullmandel

SLEEPING APARTMENTS OF KASHMEEREE MUL'S HOUSE

Drawn on Stone by L. Haghe from a Sketch by James Prinsep Esqr. Printed by C. Hullmandel

ELEVATION OF THE TEMPLE OF VISHVESHVUR AT BENARES

Drawn on Stone by L. Haghe from a Sketch by James Prinsep Esqr.
by C. Hullmandel

MUSJID NEAR RAJ GHAT, BENARES

Drawn on Stone by L. Haghe from a Sketch by James Prinsep Esqr.
Printed by C. Hullmandel